3/13

DATE DUE

MAY 0 7 2013	
AUG 2 6 2014	
OCT 0 4 2014	

TOUGH GUIDES

HOW TO SURVIVE ON A
MOUNTAIN

LOUISE SPILSBURY

PowerKiDS
press.

New York

Published in 2013 by The Rosen Publishing Group, Inc.
29 East 21st Street, New York, NY 10010

Copyright © 2013 by The Rosen Publishing Group, Inc.

Produced for Rosen by Calcium Creative Ltd
Editors for Calcium Creative Ltd: Sarah Eason and Jennifer Sanderson
US Editor: Sara Antill
Designer: Simon Borrough

Photo credits: Cover: Shutterstock: Galyna Andrushko, Eric Isselée. Inside: Dreamstime: Jolanta Dabrowska 11c, Szefei 5t; Shutterstock: Amidala76 25t, Galyna Andrushko 8l, 16cr, 18c, 20l, Bbbar 9c, Miguel Azevedo E Castro 20cl, Dennis Donohue 14c, Greg Epperson 22cl, Volodymyr Goinyk 4l, 16l, 28l, Iwona Grodzka 29l, Levent Konuk 17c, Mashe 12cr, Mikeledray 21tl, Tan Wei Ming 8c, Momentum 28c, Nyvlt-art 6l, 18l, PhotoHappiness 4r, Mikhail Pogosov 24c, Peerakit Jirachetthakun POPCITY 4c, Praseodimio 6cr, 19c, Scott E Read 15c, Sav-in 10c, Svetlana Tikhonova 13t, Leonid Tit 26c, Sergey Toronto 7tl, Bertold Werkmann 27t, Wild Arctic Pictures 23c, Yellowj 10l, 12l, 14l, 22l, 24l, 26l

Library of Congress Cataloging-in-Publication Data

Spilsbury, Louise.
 How to survive on a mountain / by Louise Spilsbury.
    p. cm. — (Tough guides)
 Includes index.
 ISBN 978-1-4488-7871-0 (library binding) — ISBN 978-1-4488-7936-6 (pbk.) —
 ISBN 978-1-4488-7942-7 (6-pack)
 1. Wilderness survival—Juvenile literature. 2. Mountaineering—Juvenile literature.
 3. Mountain ecology—Juvenile literature. I. Title.
 GV200.52.S75 2013
 796.522—dc23
                          2011052888

Manufactured in the United States of America

CPSIA Compliance Information: Batch #SW12PK: For Further Information contact Rosen Publishing, New York, New York at 1-800-237-9932

CONTENTS

SURVIVAL!

Mighty mountains can be difficult places to live in or visit. The higher up you go, the more challenging they become. When you start your climb near the bottom, the land looks like the surrounding area, with trees, plants, farms, and buildings. As you climb higher up a mountain, it gets colder, windier, and wetter.

Rocky Mountains

ROCKY MOUNTAINS
WHERE: western North America, from Alberta, Canada to New Mexico
HIGHEST POINT: Mount Elbert: 14,440 feet (4,401 m)

Hengduan Shan
mountains

When you get higher than a level called the **tree line**, there are no more trees. Here, open spaces are blasted by the wind, and plants cling to the ground where it is less windy. On **peaks** farther up, it is too cold and windy for any plants to grow. The land here is covered in bare rock, ice, and snow.

TOUGH TIP

Mountains become colder by two to three degrees Fahrenheit for each 1,000 feet that you climb. Do not venture too far up a mountain without being prepared for the icy temperatures you will find.

HENGDUAN SHAN MOUNTAINS
WHERE: Yunnan province, China
HIGHEST POINT: Mount Gongga: 24,790 feet (7,555 m)

5

KEEPING WARM

Weather can change quickly on a mountain, from warm and sunny to windy, wet, and freezing in a couple of hours. If you get too cold and wet you risk **hypothermia**. The body becomes so cold that it starts to shut down. You feel so sleepy and confused that you may not know you need help. Hypothermia can kill if it is not treated very quickly.

Dress to avoid hypothermia.

HYPOTHERMIA
SYMPTOMS: body temperature below 95° F (35° C)
ACTION: seek medical help immediately

TOUGH TIP

When **frostbite** freezes parts of the body, people cannot feel those parts anymore. In the worst cases, fingers or toes have had to be cut off. Frostbite attacks the nose, ears, cheeks, chin, fingers, or toes, so protect yourself by wearing a hat, gloves, scarf, and thick socks.

hat and scarf

To avoid hypothermia and survive icy mountain temperatures you need the right gear. That means lots of layers. The layers trap air between them and this keeps in your warmth. A jacket that is **windproof** and **waterproof** stops fierce mountain winds from making you colder, and rain from soaking into clothes beneath.

FROSTBITE
SYMPTOMS: white or grayish skin, skin that feels unusually firm or waxy, and numbness
ACTION: warm, but do not rub, the affected area

SAFE SHELTER

A mountain is no place to be out at night, even in warm and waterproof clothes. You need a shelter from the extreme cold to survive. Mountain homes have tall, sloping roofs so that heavy snow slides off them. If you are stranded on a mountain at night, put up a tent quickly or make a shelter from a fallen tree trunk covered in branches.

mountain home

MOUNTAIN HOME
WHAT: a roof's pitch is the measure of its slope
DESIGN: mountain homes have roofs with a 45 degree angle

If you are above the tree line, you may have to make a snow cave. Dig an entrance tunnel into a steep slope of snow. Then dig a room behind the entrance. The entrance tunnel should be lower than the room to stop winds from blowing into the cave. When inside, use an empty pack to block the entrance tunnel.

mountain tents

TOUGH TIP

Make a hole in the roof of your snow cave for air. Keep poking it from inside to keep it clear. Light a candle, too. A candle cannot burn without **oxygen**, so if it goes out you know you are running out of air!

MOUNTAIN TENT
WHAT: mountain winds can blow through a tent and tear it
DESIGN: a tent's **geodesic** shape means that when wind hits the side, it is directed over the tent

WILD WATER

Humans can survive for three weeks without food, but only three days without water. Even if you are really thirsty, do not eat snow. It will just make you colder. Instead light a fire and melt snow into water. Water from high, fast-flowing mountain streams is usually safe to drink.

stream

MOUNTAIN STREAM
WHAT: freshwater for drinking
USE: more than half the world's people rely on mountain water to drink, grow food, to produce electricity, and to supply industries

TOUGH TIP

Some snakes swim in streams or hide in rocks or plants nearby. Watch where you are walking and use a stick to roll stones out of the way if you have to. Avoid all snakes, even harmless-looking ones, just in case they are **poisonous**.

Lower down a mountain, streams flow more slowly and may form pools. Beware! This water may be dirty or have leeches in it. Leeches are black, swimming worms that latch onto your body and suck your blood. Boil water before you drink it to kill leeches. If you swallow them alive, they can give you sores inside your body.

leech

LEECH
SIZE: grows up to 8 inches (20 cm) long
THREAT: sharp teeth make a Y-shaped bite and their saliva (spit) numbs the wound while they suck out blood

FINDING FOOD

Y ou need food to survive. Insects are a good source of protein and you should be able to find worms, millipedes, and other minibeasts under logs. Avoid centipedes because they bite!

trout

TOUGH TIP

To catch a fish, build two **dams** in a stream to create a pool. Get a stick and try to hit a fish with it. Even if you miss, the splash might stop the fish long enough for you to flip it out onto the bank.

TROUT
SIZE: adult trout can be 8 inches (20 cm) to 4 feet (1.2 m) long
USE: eating 3 ounces (85 g) of fish gives you about 144 **calories**

juniper berries

Fish from mountain rivers are great to eat when cooked over a fire. They are also very good for you. Many wild mountain berries taste delicious, but some are poisonous. The key is to eat only the wild berries that look like ones you know. Mountain blueberries, strawberries, blackberries, and raspberries are small but they look and taste like store-bought berries.

JUNIPER BERRIES
TASTE: bitter when eaten raw
USE: cooked in foods and sauces to add flavor

DANGEROUS ANIMALS

Wild and dangerous animals lurk on mountains. Cougars are large, powerful cats with deadly claws and a killer bite. They hide among rocks or plants and leap out suddenly to swipe **prey** with their claws. They avoid humans but if you meet one, stand very still. If you run, it will chase you!

cougar

COUGAR
SIZE: grows to 4 feet (1.2 m) long, weighs up to 140 pounds (63 kg)
THREAT: sneaks up on prey, then leaps out suddenly

Grizzly bears are huge and very strong. Their massive, flat paws have long, deadly claws and their teeth can crush bone. One swipe from a bear paw can kill you. Grizzly bears eat mostly plants, but they will break into cars or rip open tents to steal human food. They may also attack if you meet them in the wild.

I SURVIVED

When a grizzly bear suddenly ran at 32-year-old Timothy Hix, he knew what he had to do to survive. He dropped to the ground, covered his head, and remained still. The bear bit him a couple times and pawed him, but then it lost interest and just walked away.

grizzly bear

GRIZZLY BEAR
SIZE: grows to 8 feet (2.4 m) long, weighs up to 900 pounds (408 kg)
THREAT: runs fast and often attacks to defend cubs

15

LIVING THE HIGH LIFE

As you go higher up a mountain, there is less and less oxygen in the air. If you climb too high too quickly, your body cannot breathe in as much oxygen as it needs. You can get headaches, run out of breath, and have trouble thinking clearly. Some people black out. This is called **altitude sickness** and it can be very dangerous.

The Himalayas

THE HIMALAYAS
WHERE: Asia, along border between India and Tibet
HIGHEST POINT: Mount Everest: 29,035 feet (8,849 m)

If you get altitude sickness, walk or climb down to a lower level on the mountain. You should recover in a day or two. Some people have to use an oxygen tank to get the extra oxygen they need. People with very bad altitude sickness may have to be rescued by helicopter.

TOUGH TIP

To avoid altitude sickness, go up slowly, take it easy, and give your body time to get used to the change in height. Sleep at a spot that is lower than you were during the day. This will help your body to get used to the shortage of oxygen.

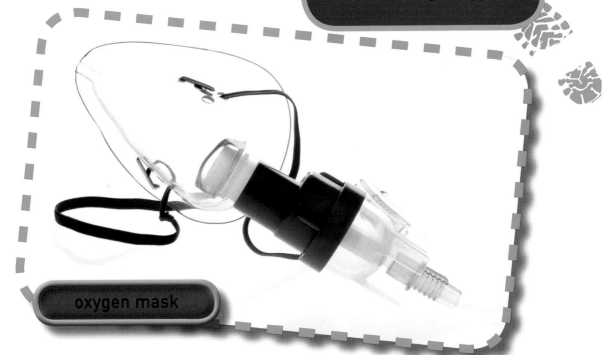

oxygen mask

OXYGEN MASK
WHAT: contains a tube with oxygen
USE: face mask is placed over the altitude sickness victim's mouth and nose to deliver oxygen

BURNING SUN

Sun shining off mountain snow is beautiful, but dangerous. Your skin can burn more quickly at the top of a mountain than it does on a sunny beach. That is because thin mountain air lets through more **ultraviolet rays**, or UV rays. Also, snow reflects the Sun's rays, so the Sun hits you twice!

mountain top

SNOW
WHAT: snow on a mountain top does not melt
WHY: reflects 90 percent of the sunlight that falls on it

To avoid burning your skin, cover it up and use a strong sunblock to protect your face and lips. Wear a pair of wraparound sunglasses or goggles. These prevent **snow blindness**, when your eyes get damaged by the Sun. Snow blindness is painful and can cause permanent damage.

I SURVIVED

Minutes after reaching the peak of Mount Everest, Brian Dickinson got snow blindness. He had dropped and cracked his goggles on the way up and the Sun shining off the snow had burned his eyes. Slipping and tumbling as he went, Dickinson managed to feel his way down to safety by clinging onto **guide ropes**.

snow goggles

SNOW GOGGLES
WHAT: made of material that stops UV rays from damaging eyes
DESIGN: large so eyes are always protected. Goggles also have features that stop them from fogging up.

FINDING YOUR WAY

When snow falls and covers rocks and other **landmarks**, it is hard to tell where you are. To survive and find your way to safety you need a map and a compass. You can use distant landmarks, such as mountain peaks and faraway lakes, to find yourself on the map. A compass will lead you in the right direction.

map and compass

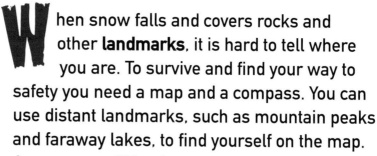

COMPASS
WHAT: tool for finding direction
HOW: needle of a compass always points north

If you get lost, send signals to help people find you. Choose an open area away from trees and spread out any colored gear you can spare. You could collect damp wood and start a fire. The damp wood gives off a lot of smoke that airplanes and **search parties** can spot from far away.

fire signal

I SURVIVED

Imagine being separated from your family and lost on a snow-covered mountain at nightfall. That happened to 14-year-old Jake Denham. Luckily Jake remembered a survival trick he saw on a television program. He followed ski trails left by skiers down the mountain until he met up with mountain rescuers.

FIRE SIGNAL
HOW: start fire with dry grass or sticks and add bigger pieces of wood as it burns
SAFETY: build fire 6 feet (182 cm) away from **flammable** objects

HIDDEN DANGERS

Many mountain climbers have lost their lives by falling suddenly into a deep, open crack in mountain ice called a **crevasse**. The position of these dangerous holes changes every year because crevasses form in enormous blocks of ice, called **glaciers**, which move very slowly downhill.

climbing ropes

CLIMBING ROPES
SIZE: up to 4 inches (10 cm) thick and 200 feet (61 m) long
USE: climbers are tied together so they can grip onto the mountain if one falls

When snow falls in winter, crevasses are often covered and hidden by snow that forms a bridge over the gap. In warmer weather, these snow bridges start to melt and become weak. They create a deadly, invisible trap for climbers and skiers who can easily fall deep inside the crevasses below them.

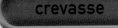

crevasse

CREVASSE
SIZE: up to 65 feet (20 m) wide, 150 feet (45 m) deep, 1,300 feet (405 m) long
THREAT: steep, icy sides make it very hard to climb out of a crevasse

AVALANCHE!

Avalanches are banks of snow that slide down mountains without any warning. They race as fast as an express train and roar like a thunderstorm. They can crush things in their way or bury them under a thick blanket of snow. Avalanche breakers are strong walls or fences that hold back avalanches.

avalanche

AVALANCHE
SPEED: can travel as fast as 80 miles per hour (128 km/h)
THREAT: kills about 150 people in North America and Europe a year

rescue dog

If an avalanche hits you, it feels like being tossed around in a dryer full of snow and ice. People trapped in an avalanche can get buried under snow or injured when they knock into things inside the snow. Some people carry a life-saving rucksack with an air bag inside. When the air bag fills with air, it keeps you on the surface of the avalanche so you are not crushed by the snow.

TOUGH TIP

If you are hit by an avalanche, "swim" with your arms to stay near the surface. If you are trapped when the avalanche stops, quickly make an air space with your hands in front of your face so you can breathe until rescue comes.

RESCUE DOGS
WHAT: one dog can do the job of 20 human searchers
HOW: can smell, hear, and feel the movements of people trapped under snow

25

LIGHTNING STRIKES

Mountain peaks are especially dangerous during a storm because lightning strikes the highest object in an area. Flashes of lightning can burn and sometimes kill if they hit people. If you can see or hear lightning on a mountaintop, you are close enough to be a target for these bolts of energy.

lightning

LIGHTNING
TEMPERATURE: the air around a bolt of lightning is about 54,000° F (29,982° C), which is hotter than the surface of the Sun
THREAT: people can die if they are struck by lightning

lightning arresters

TOUGH TIP

Do not take chances. Check the weather forecast before you go on a mountain trip and make sure you are off high places before a storm arrives. Hike early in the day and make sure you are down by lunchtime because most mountain storms happen in the afternoon.

If you are stranded on a mountain top when a storm hits, get below the tree line as fast as you can! Try to get inside a building or car, or under the shade of a thick forest of trees. If you are in an open space, crouch down with only your feet touching the ground. Keep your feet close together and ride out the storm.

LIGHTNING ARRESTER
WHAT: rod that carries electricity from lightning into the ground
USE: attached to the roofs of mountain buildings to stop lightning from damaging buildings or injuring people

STAYING SAFE

Mountains can be challenging places but they can provide all you need for survival if you know where to look. You can drink the clear, freshwater in fast-flowing streams and rivers. You can make shelters from wood and even snow. You can eat wild berries and catch river fish to cook over a wood fire.

climbing group

CLIMBING GROUP
WHY: climbing a mountain alone is risky
ACTION: join an organized group with an experienced leader

One way to make sure you return safely from a mountain trip is to be prepared. Mountain experts take a basic survival kit with them at all times, packed in a waterproof container in their backpack.

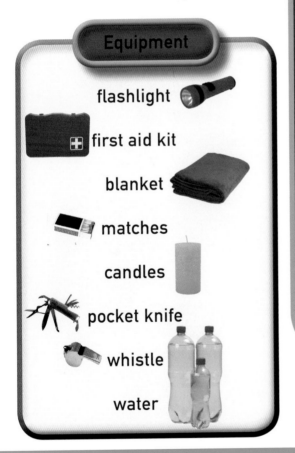

Equipment

flashlight

first aid kit

blanket

matches

candles

pocket knife

whistle

water

TOUGH TIP

Things to take:

- A map and a compass
- A flashlight with extra batteries
- Sun protection and goggles
- Extra clothing
- Extra water and dried food
- A small first aid kit
- A sharp pocket knife
- A loud whistle and **flares** for signaling
- Waterproof matches and candles
- Rope or cord
- A large, bright plastic bag for shelter or for signaling

EMERGENCY WHISTLE
WHAT: used to signal for help
HOW: the internationally recognized distress signal is six long blasts repeated at one minute intervals

GLOSSARY

altitude sickness (AL-tuh-tood SIK-nes) An illness caused by a lack of oxygen.

calories (KA-luh-rees) Units that measure how much energy a food gives you.

crevasse (krih-VAS) A deep. open crack in a glacier.

dams (DAMZ) Barriers built across rivers.

flammable (FLAH-muh-bul) Easily catches fire.

flares (FLAYRZ) Signaling devices that make a short, bright flame.

frostbite (FROST-byt) When part of the body is damaged by cold.

geodesic (jee-uh-DEH-sik) Shaped so that wind passes easily over.

glaciers (GLAY-shurz) Large masses of ice formed by snow on a mountain.

guide ropes (GYD ROHPS) Ropes pinned to the mountain to help climbers find their way.

hypothermia (hy-puh-THUR-mee-uh) When the body's temperature is too low.

landmarks (LAND-marks) Things you see from a distance that help you to know where you are.

oxygen (OK-sih-jen) A gas in the air that humans need to breathe to live.

peaks (PEEKS) The pointed tops of mountains.

poisonous (POYZ-nus) Something that can kill if swallowed.

prey (PRAY) An animal that is hunted and eaten by other animals.

search parties (SERCH PAR-teez) Rescuers who search for lost people.

snow blindness (SNOH BLYND-nes) Temporary blindness caused by light reflecting off snow.

tree line (TREE LYN) The level on a mountain above which trees do not grow.

ultraviolet rays (ul-truh-VY-uh-let RAYZ) Rays given off by the Sun that can hurt your skin and eyes.

waterproof (WAH-ter-proof) Keeps out water.

windproof (WIND-proof) Keeps out wind.

FURTHER READING

Hodge, Susie. *Mountain Survival.* Extreme Habitats. New York: Gareth
    Stevens, 2008.

Sandler, Michael. *Mountains: Surviving on Mt. Everest.* X-treme Places.
    New York: Bearport Publishing, 2006.

Shone, Rob. *Defying Death in the Mountains.* Graphic Survival Stories.
    New York: Rosen Publishing, 2010.

WEBSITES

Due to the changing nature of Internet links, PowerKids Press has
developed an online list of websites related to the subject of this book.
This site is updated regularly. Please use this link to access the list:
www.powerkidslinks.com/guide/mount/

INDEX